Lifting Myself
By My Own Toes

poems by

BD Feil

Finishing Line Press
Georgetown, Kentucky

Lifting Myself
By My Own Toes

ACKNOWLEDGMENTS

Poems in this collection have been nominated for Pushcart Prizes as well as
appearing in journals like *Poet Lore, Slice Magazine, The Penn Review, New Plains
Review, Margie,* and *Plainsongs.*

Publisher: Leah Huete de Maines
Editor: Christen Kincaid
Cover Art: BD Feil
Author Photo: BD Feil
Cover Design: Elizabeth Maines McCleavy

Order online: www.finishinglinepress.com
also available on amazon.com

Author inquiries and mail orders:
Finishing Line Press
P. O. Box 1626
Georgetown, Kentucky 40324
U. S. A.

Table of Contents

(red-knuckled apples)

(now is the time for the sighing)

(well-meaning strokes)

Words

This was explained to me once so that
it's stayed with me past memory
then just a child painful in silence
in eyeful aversion some weren't sure
I was even there told most likely
matter-of-factly maybe dropped casually
like trivia oh this could be of some use
some day or here this might be good to know
before all the words fell into shadow
and dark streets were either dreamed
or wandered I could never tell which
but then those words made perfect sense
right when they were spoken so much so
that I remember not knowing how I
could go on without them I took them
inside and lived every day after with them
I must have
I just can't remember them now
those words from then
not at all

Noli Timere

The garden is this way
the path that meanders in a straight line
stick to it but don't follow it
the way in is not the way out
walk backward to move forward
keep your eyes closed
revel in today
before you know it the sun will set
and your hopes like bats will go a-flyin'
not a sail big enough to catch them all
at the top of the hill is your cubicle
the desk is yours
some drawers open
some don't
it depends on the hour
the tilt of the sun
the humidity
there is no downpayment
however there is a deposit
feel free to rock yourself to sleep
fall if you must but do so quietly
drifting lightly side to side
we hope you're not hurt
do not be afraid

That Is This

There are the Words. And then
there is their sister Memory
who is never really seen
only talked of incessantly
described in high detail
chatted up and down into
something as fierce and beautiful
as the piercing sun in the sky
a thing not to be looked at
directly and even then
you can't really she being only
rumor or legend or at least
has become so through her brothers
who are everywhere bragging
although there is something else
not Words and not Memory something
standing sideways in the sunlight
sideways in the streams of speech
so you can't quite make out its
true shape. And that is this.

Judgment Day

And in the end there was no end
all revelation finding employment elsewhere
prophecy assigned winding queues
looped through the workaday week
horded pork-n-beans half-life Little Debbies
nine-to-fives then seven-to-tens
all idle numerology swallowed
by halves and chunks
into the crank and grind
making it through the day and then
another and then Lordknew

Courage

That chance is gone if it was ever here.
Though I doubt my nature would have let it in,
Refusing as it did to wipe its feet.
But when I was young I wish I had the courage
To fall flat in the mire, to throw all in,
To glide and sink with the winds, to fall back
With eyes wide, to not worry, mostly
Of numbers and bread, of all matter of things.
Of sadness.
To not panic about love, nor be so sure
That I knew what failure looked like.
I wish I were not so quick to strike a line through experience.
I was young, after all.   I knew nothing.
And in this I should have reveled like a hog in mud.

Cane Deferred

From closet gloaming it looks out.
As hesitant as you. A drop less
Malice. Knobbed and grained and knotted,
That one-eyed crook
Leaning lonely and cornered, avoided
For the most part. Deferred from fear of fear.

In form, just a stick, found
Appendage of a tree. No shame in a stick.
Birds feel none and less.
A simple machine. A lever of sorts.
A prop is all, kickstands life.
Blessed branch. Easy. Only,
Don't expect miracles.

To expect solution is to expect magic,
The click-clack of incantation.
To expect magic, then dumb
Melodrama. Flowing robes and greasepaint.
A wave Hestonianly over Sea.
Behold! Deliverance from Pharaoh!

So try the right hand first. The left has its
Own rhythm. Always has.
Pauses and stutters, cadence like a cicada,
The long trill-song unconnected
To stumbles. There. Feel it. You can feel it
Up in the knob as it strikes the ground.
A beat, a kind of code-cry.

Talk to it, then, like an old dog on the Fourth
Cringing from far-off cracks
Booms and rockets, driving the poor
Mad thing to the very edge.
It might do no good
But it will pass the time.

And time, that creep, is the enemy after all.
You need all the allies you can gather.

Nothingness

Already we've lost it if we must
Put a name to it, if we tilt the machine
To our favors, force dogged tabs into slots,
If we insist upon nomenclature.

It's no longer that crystalline thing.
But then, it never was that thing, that thing
Of primary color or right angle or straight
Line, anything of matter, any of thing.

Well, even now I don't define it, do I?
It circles back into circle, and there
I go again. It is the thing impossible
To be named. Yes, it is the impossible.

Tender Bits

As in all things that matter
in fights at meals with love
in playing the villain
go for the tender bits
seek them out
find their sanctuaries
hurl yourself directly on
head down with all resolution
grab them
hold on doggedly
snap at them with graced fervor
bite down in ancient faith
with all art and flourish
do it heartily and savor

Taking The Thing For A Swim

Rolled on my back, kicked my legs.
Easy, frog-like, learned in Tadpoles.
At least not untaught. Never graduated.
Took the thing gently on to my chest.
Gave it easy rides around the water.
It faced my face. I could see it was rattled,
Unsure, both of balance and liquid.
Maybe of its vessel, too. And I was unsure
Of it. Dog? Weasel? Mole? Varmint?
Did it matter? Does it matter now?

A dream-creature. A dreamer far from home.

What I'm trying to say is that I tried to ease its mind,
To get it to see the goodness of the water,
The peace of the strokes, rudimentary
Yet hypnotic, clumsy yet well-meaning.

Well, what is well-meaning? Safe. A kind of love.

Professions

As Librarians
are always
the loudest,
Hangmen
the most content,
Gangsters
the most just,
Saints
by far
the pettiest,
so you are,
my Friend,
the cruelest.

Leftover Sonnet

Too many bras on backs of doors
too many motel towels bulging drawers
too many potato peelers
too many nutcrackers
too many corkscrews
love's too much while we're at it
the big ball of rubber bands was ill-conceived and stupid
but time inside our icebox dances
cold pizza trumps hot
picnic chicken basketed for hours
lords it over fowl just lifted from the fryer
next morning's meatloaf sandwich is nobody's fool
       luxurious gropings in darkness
        cohabitation in lightless refrigeration

And Yet

And yet it comes on
oh silent for the most part
without apparent movement
I might say like a minute hand
or a small dune
on the edge of an oak woods
or even that far
corner of the room
that looks the same
day in and day out
oh but you say that far
corner does not move
and yet it comes on

A Reading

I read you all wrong
put you in a city attic
looking out across blocks and roofs
listening to sirens
to downstairs lovers
when all the time you were tending
the long rows of broad beans
watching peasants hurry to mass
hearing crows mock the day

let me back up start again
it makes all the difference
legitimizes experience
oh not yours you're fine
the fault is always mine
a quickness to declare a taste
that heaviest of burdens
a clown in a routine
trying to lift himself by his own toes

(savages and monsters)

Something Like A River

Always it should be like a river, yes,
Flowing and continuous, yes, steady
And unconscious like time and timeless, too,
Like two old shoes tied together
Twisting in too cold current,
But also mean, also ruthless,
Bypassing the fetidness of theory,
Quick to no real point, overflowing
And obliterating levees and lives,
Too inhospitable for pleasure craft,
Too uncomfortable for tourists.
Oh, all this, but don't forget open,
Open to the indescribable,
Meandering nowhere in a lazy way, la!
Malleable and soft, caving in
To the obviousness of the light,
Giving way with gratitude to the truth,
To the backwash of the sea,
The sea.
But, yes, always like a river.

Heaven

So here now, a version to leave you with.
In commiseration, for comfort even.
Myself, I must be going, don't get up.
But go ahead, pick the setting, however
Paradisiacal. Gauzy clouds will do.
Too green fields, tranquil surf and sand.
They're in the best brochures. Needless to say,
All white and breezy, in which case
Pick up togas from Wardrobe.
But there we will all meet, forever and ever
And ever again. The loved ones and family,
The friends and friendly, the confidants and
Confessors, once loomed so large
In our hours. Missing, now found. Though
Who knows the caprices of heaven?
And though we might nod, hail and glad-hand,
We'll do it vaguely and warily, off-center,
Like a squint from a distant hill.
All whos deemed superfluous.
ID realized overrated.
Credential washed with the tide.
Oh, surely Our Nirvana should be set,
Eternal and perfect, while we wander freely,
Walk deeply on floating beaches,
Sip the pure air of balanced humidity.
Yet there we are contemplating faces,
Curiously loving whomever we pass,
Forever drifting, confused, in loose-fitting fabric.

Night

In those the early days—dumb, yes,
Simple and brute, curious and poking
But only as far as the fire—
We feared the night. All light taken from us,
All warmth, as if we were being punished.
Just what had we done? So we invented.
Persecuted. Stigmatized. Found religion.
Still, toward evening, nerves jangled, things dimmed.
Extinction seemed imminent. There were
The great moan-songs, much panic, gnashing
Of teeth, tearing of hair, running in
Those circles we now recognize as prayer.

Until some of us who preferred standing-off,
Lingering at the edge of things, watchful
And very quiet, tilting our heads
At the horizon in what then passed
For deep thought, began accepting the dark,
Loving the night, embracing the things that winked
And whistled, laughed and whispered. We waited
For the dark as we waited for lovers. This, all
After the sun fell from the sky, cursing us.
We sold our souls then to the unseen.
Plumbed our trust into blackest night.
Took comfort in forsaken oblivion.

Cat

I have a perfectly good name for him
and he comes when I call that name
though he comes too when I merely step
from the back door without food or water
he can see nothing gets past him
it's possible that what I call him
isn't his real name at all that he simply
comes because he's happy to see me
a nice thought
most likely if I knew his real name
I wouldn't be able to pronounce it anyway
lacking proper larynx and spit and fangs
besides maybe he holds his true name
in close to his heart like something sacred
or dear only used by his mother so long ago
an even nicer thought
still it could be that when he first sees me
when he runs across the garden to me
when he ekes out a kind of *ack-ack*
consistently and loudly for all to hear
he thinks this is my name and perhaps
I will perk up my ears and feel a little lost
and sad for a sound from so long ago

Produce

An accumulation
of grievance over
the accession of summer
somehow cheated out of
a fair share of cherries
kept from my rightful
portion of sweet corn
in lieu of ripe melon
hearts I eat out my own
but heaven is coming
I'll bring the hoe
churn it all up
sow what is owed
saints and angels be damned
body and blood
in grain and loam

O, Savagery

Without moral compass, shame, parsimony,
 In summer we gorge on fruit, abundant and cheap.
At times overripe. They are here. Now.
We don't care, we are careless.
Rinds tossed over shoulders, off porches,
Into great cracking bonfires around which,
If our bellies were not so swollen,
We would dance, knees to chins, fingers snapping.

Instead we sit back, slumped, juices
Running from our mouths, forging divergent paths
Down around nipples, reservoiring in navels
Momentarily, complacently, dreamily,
Before overflowing, resuming south across
Bare thighs, disappearing into nethers,
A lost world, prehistoric, best forgotten.
We may or may not swallow the seeds, who knows?

Song Of The Horaltic

I've gone up ahead I could not wait
yesterday the trees intrigued to lose their leaves
all at once and all for good
a bright day little wind
I watched them conspiring in silence
a soul then is what you make of it I shrugged
but I stepped no further surmised no more

today the collar claws the sackcloth rubs
today the blood surges
today I lose my clothes my reason my only self
surely I leap oh surely I bound
surely beyond this lawn
beyond this groomed devil's strip
beyond this season's moans and motives
some fallow clearing rises
some hill if I dare heap on hope
one dead tree jagged stark and lonely
where I can rest without cold pursuit
and there strike my horaltic pose
as sweat dries and hardens to armor on my back

and there idle time away
to wait the sun to bake my downy nape
to breathe in the patterned ideals
to set right the tilt of my crown
to set straight my turned feathers
to cast my noble chin
to gain some glory some substance
some little space
I've gone up ahead I could not wait

This Is What She Said She Saw

She said it was like watching a tree fall,
Like watching a tree fall slowly, stop-frame,
Spring, a wet warm Winter, nothing to hold dear,
The ground all around soft and yielding,
A tree, slowly tilting, tearing its divot
Of root and ragged earth in one great heave,
Branches grasping at the sky,
Birds hanging on till the last bit
Playing chicken with a sure thing,
Only to skip, off, up, out of the branches
Nonchalantly on to the next tree,
The next life, with no more fuss than side-stepping
From curb to street, as they flew from my hair,
As the dogs crossed me up and down I went,
Slowly but majestically, like a tree, she said.

February Loans

My hair this morning from titmouse
my whiskers from squirrel
my reek of wet wandering dog
pockets bulge with nuts foraged berries pecked
somewhere in here mangled mouse
my ego up with rough-legged hawk
soaring left right ignorant of bald eagle above
bald hunter in fire sumac below
my worry dripping gutter
my vainglory blue jay
my obstinance Canadian goose
my mania ubiquitous wind
tundra everywhere hard dominant blank

Monster

I know they're in there, Dad. I just know it.
I can feel them. This I catch as I fall
In behind them, or they fall in ahead of me.
The three of us going in the same direction
But not quite together. The boy explaining,
The father nodding, and me giving space
But too close in pace to escape their words.
The boy trying to place each word just-so
Between the others. *But I tell myself*
There can't be any, can't be any in my closet,
Can there, Dad? He forms each word with care,
As carefully as he places each small foot
In the soft sand stretching ahead of us.

I listen as the father nods, listen as the words
Imprint on the father's face as the boy says,
But I just know it, Dad. I know there are monsters,
His head tipped in explanation to
The lapping water,
His hands twisting in a cat's cradle
Of clarity, his voice working to be heard
Until his father asks, W*ell, have you seen*
Any? Have you seen any monsters?
The boy's face. The father's face.
Both their foot prints in the sand. The sand smooth
But only ahead of them. Me stepping,
Listening to their prints, to each of their words.
The father not so much hearing as trying
To understand, as trying to make right,
As trying to fix.

And now both their faces cast down, fixed
Intently on sand, on each other's words.
And I think it must be respect keeping them walking,
Keeping us all three of pace, the space constant
Between the boy, the father, and me.
No, I haven't seen any actual

Monsters, but the thing is, Dad, I feel them.
The father silent.
The lapping water.
I know they're in there, that's the thing.
And I think, yes, it is respect.
But also worry. The father can't help
But be worried. Not for monsters—
Oh, we know there are none—
But worried he can't make right, can't make smooth
All the stretching sand the boy walks on.
And I want to say from behind, *No you can't,*
Though I'm only listening, *not really.*
Besides, he knows that.
The lapping water.
The cry of a gull far out and above.

I slow to give them a step, and they slow,
Too, until the father says, Listen.
There are no monsters. Silence. *There are no*
Such things as monsters. More silence. *But you know that.*
Then more silence and for a long time after.
The lapping water.
Then the father says, *Although,* and here
I want to say, *Please don't,* or do I blurt it out?
Stop. Don't say more. But on he stumbles.
Yes, sometimes. Sometimes you can feel them.
But he says this in a hurry,
As if he's not sure he should, as if
This might be too much for the boy, as if
This might be the one thing his son takes away.
The beach. The sand. The foot prints.
The cry of the gull far out and above.
Not the denial of monsters, not their banishment
And slaying and laying low by this knight-comforter,
This good father trying to smooth the way,
But their awful acknowledgement. *Yes, you can*
Always feel them. You can always in a way feel them.

And the boy listens a long time in the silence
That curves with the shore.
The lapping water.
The lapping water.

But it's clear to me now from where I keep pace
That the boy is worried, worried that his father
Might have gone too far, stumbled too much along
Into truth, and it's the boy now who will need
To comfort, to be the one to make right,
To fix. *Yes, but the monsters*, he says,
They're not really there right, Dad?
Not really? And here I can feel the father's
Burden lift, feel his gratitude toward his son
For pointing the way across the smooth sand,
And he says, *Yes.* Then, *Or I mean, no.*
Then he splits the difference, *No, they're not really*
There, but yes, you can feel them. And he hesitates.
At least you think you can. Then more silence.

And here the boy realizes that this might be
The best he's going to get, at least so it seems
To me, pulled along as I am behind them,
And he says, *Well, I can feel them, that's all.*
Then nothing more. And there's no sound.
Not the cry of a gull far out and above
Or the lapping water
Or our six spaced feet scuffing the smooth sand.
Until the boy says, under his breath,
But, mostly, I feel like they're always listening.
And the father nods, and we walk on in silence, mostly.

Panorama

Such checks on human sight, cheekbones
And eye sockets, the blurry bridge of my nose,
The mossy ledge of my brow, thick locks
And bangs when I had hair. The only thing
Sure now, narrow and underfoot, dogspaws
In the snow, there, to and from the fenced yard
Twice a day, regular, faithful. Though beyond
I hear the bare rumors of holy things,
Bone-memory lingering at the edges.

Let's see, I know woods fill my right
And noisy wetlands my left, and behind these,
Nearly certain, a railroad curving off
By roar and whistle down to a river
That leads in its amble-meander
To a bay, rounded and ample, space
Enough for all the ships to lay
A-wait in serene-arcs for the wind
To furl and nudge them out to sea

Surely these pictures neat—illustrations
By Wyeth, full pages, spaced regular—
Fit snug enough. And enough is as good
As a feast. Enough. My circle rounds on me,
Grows tighter each day. Do I dare consider
The years? Light throws up walls like anything.
Travels considered then dismissed,
Adventures recalled but never landed. Still,
I know the horizon, I know it's there.

Hollyhocks

Their flowers
the pastels of crocheted
hats old women craft
to hide their toilet rolls
their leaves laid waste to lace
at once by unctuous beetles
for them no bye from the dying
no immunity from the failing
each year starting over again
volunteering without draft
ready like a fresh roll
under a tiny hat

Exile

Put me by the Sea, lonely windswept crag,
Foamy steps descending into brine.

If not the Sea, then high above a Great Lake,
Lead me down in chains as I sing low-song.

Or a River swift, audible and effervescent.
I need to hear current over me.

At least stake me under a tree as I decay,
Rain rolling from one leaf to another

Down on to taut skin, waiting skin.
Failing these, if still they blame me,

Prop open my cell window so
Thru-traffic and sirens can waft in,

The hubbub of crowds, the cries of protest,
All the water-babble, voices, sighs.

This Chill

This is too bad this weather
too bad this rain this chill
these dropping leaves these clouds
slung so low you feel their fingers
plucking your hair like old boney aunts

one goose heads more east than south
lost from formation or just lost
jumping from old water to new
thinking this is the place I was before
thinking there is a better place I go

this truck makes its circles
helpless to do otherwise
away and then back away and then
always returning to four thankless walls
like Thoreau I bring home the laundry

in this chill truth hides its smile
old men hunker in frosted silence
beauty cast adrift all direction lost
god is everywhere we refuse to go
god is everything we refuse to know

In Which Mrs. Adams Observes And Passes Judgment On The Cottonwood And The Goldfinch

Nothing bedevils Mrs. Adams more in Her useful backyard than
the cottonwood and the goldfinch every stone its purpose every animal
    its function every leaf its position every root its place under the soil
the sky above the ground underfoot the cows that moo three doors down
    the devilish crows that perch and peck despite Mrs. Adams' oaths to
off off off the cantaloupe that sprawls into the peas that climb
    the sunflowers that hang their sad heads over the rabbits that sit
just beyond stone's throw beyond the large lady's judgments
    staring into nothing because that is what they do that is what they mean
though that is not what Mrs. Adams does or means this not Her way
    Her way the hard way of stewardship Her way the way of purpose

She knows knows well She hesitated too long early on with this
cottonwood too long into Her stewardship too long after taking
    over this weight of Nature this Her garden and now the cottonwood
is too big too big for this life She's built up all around it too big
    for the portion assigned it too close to the outbuildings that mark time
in Mrs. Adams' weighty life so likewise She observes the goldfinch
    and yet not likewise the goldfinch this yellow scamp that poses
with no purpose other than to flit no purpose other than to fly
    in and out at will and without purpose yes true partaking
of the thistle yes true partaking of the sunflower partaking
    of the berries of the black and the rasp and the winter but

is this purpose is this reason is this life is this Her way
something about the cottonwood enlarging and overwhelming
    without thought or reason something about the goldfinch's freedom
to dart without catch or cage a cocky squire of its own estate though
    not its estate it Mrs. Adams' backyard it Her garden it Her estate
thus She sits looking out ruminating all Her burdens but especially
    the cottonwood and the goldfinch not on haunches thus like a cat
because that is not Her bent but thus a little forward supplying
    Her own straight back supplying Her own spine Herself
Mrs. Adams like Her fathers before Her observing all before Her
    all She can forbear the audacious height of the cottonwood the vibrant
color of the goldfinch neither of this world neither of Her nature

thus the cottonwood neither lovely nor charming only present
every morning taller despite Her wishes thus the goldfinch praised
        for its pleasing plumage a gaudy clotheshorse despite Mrs. Adams'
modesty thus the cottonwood listed on the bottle of Ortho a subsidiary
        of Scotts-Miracle Gro as an invasive thus the goldfinch a rolling
rollicking acrobat pecking upside down over its shoulder at sunflower
        heads thus the cottonwood no evident brightness leaves like thick
plastic plates simply and efficiently turning brown plummeting to
        the ground thud just missing the goldfinch the little limber fool
who sidesteps with such ease as to shock the Very Mrs. Adams

        yes rankling and ruffling Mrs. Adams because even the late
Mr. Adams had his proper place yes a time to live yes a time to
        die yes a time for all things and so Mr. Adams passed and so the soil
in need of alkaline his ashes spread out among the cucumbers
        and the greens but also yes to drive away the dreaded cabbage loopers
and scare the rabbits in the bargain and now Mrs. Adams ponders
        the problems of Her garden the problems of Her backyard the problems
of all that She sees because all that She sees is all yes all Her charge
        She the most responsible of the species with the sin of purpose laid
at Her feet the sloth of the cottonwood towering above Her the pride
        of the goldfinch flitting around Her both rankling as they do

        until She slaps the armrest in resolve and resolves as only
Mrs. Adams resolves with auger and rope hammer and steel
        and holes bored on through the heart of the thing clean and straight
as Mrs. Adams is wont as Her fathers were wont through to the other
        side of the thing rope knotted trim and taut with ancestral ease
and there She resolves reposing till the end of the season and a week
        beyond Her full worth measured out and paid up from the cottonwood
its straight trunk pierced through with a bolt holding one end
        of the hammock bearing Mrs. Adams the other end dipping
and rising but for the most part steady on the waves of wind held by
        the goldfinch whose quick wings flutter under its steward's burden

Hangers-On

Among these remaining leaves, these stubborn
Hangers-on, these mal-lingering houseguests,
There are those who will never fall, waiting
It out through all bluster, hanging around
To keep me company, or so they say,
Always claiming it's all for my own good
But, truthfully, just not taking the hint,
Brown curled things prodding the sunwarm by
Willful ignorance, trying too hard with
Deaf fluttering chatter, washing dishes
Already washed, cracking my few good ones,
Oh, meaning well, always just meaning well,
Emptying ashtrays with the newly lit,
Straightening the empty thoughts propped open
Everywhere for my future cross-reference,
Not hip that soon they will be severed by
Their own stems, pushed out by new buds, forcing
Me into small talk all over again.

(red-knuckled apples)

Memory

Many things I remember
they insist I shouldn't
the old trestle bridge on Main Street
skating in the Green Mill
the milk wagon drawn
by the last horse in town
its slow clop echoing each morning
the hard life along the flooded river
the city before streets when swamp
covered everything to be
all my future memory
my mother cradling me after a fall
talking softly until I cried it out
oh my brothers and sisters
have always been so jealous

Birthday

I was a child of winter.
Red-knuckled apple
Left hanging till the end.
Born on the final Ides
Or close enough.
A steady paranoia
Of being cheated
By the nearness of Christmas,
The overbearance of good cheer.

Usually, it is a bleak day.
Nero shares it.

Katterheinrich

Those great uncles left the gentle harvest
Of west Ohio, the easy scything
In knee-high waves of wheat-grass, the good draft
Horses diligently pulling the plows
And reapers and threshers, the cows chewing
Fodder in lazy circular motions,
Giving all too gladly when asked nicely,
Coaxed with friendly fingers, and when violence
Necessitated, the sausage-making
Even down to the blutwurst, though that deep
In the process their young stomachs had turned,
And watermelons slept in the creek beds,
And eggs could always be found whenever
A hen slipped the recent past and simply
Walked away clucking, and they all went for
Soldiers in the Great War, all four of them,
But first changed their names to Katterhenry
So that they would not be cursed or beaten
Or burnt out or worse before they even
Boarded the transports to ship back across
The sea of their parents, before Bellau
Wood or Château-Thierry, before they stood
Lifetimes below top soil in mucked trenches
On the opposite side the Line from their
Kitchen language, though each one came back to
The farm, proved, I suppose, braver, I guess,
But free now to change back their names, or not,
Even a couple gassed for good measure
And always remembering from over
There a kind of different scything, a kind
Of different sausage-making, and their young
Gentle stomachs turned over once again.

Business Trip

I asked well
wasn't it a pain travelling so much
when we were young
when your family was growing
when your wife waited at home for your return
and he said yes
at least I think he said yes
and I just didn't drop it
in the top of my head
like a kiss on the forehead
the way a father does a son sometime
out of the wide ocean blue
and he said well
it replaced a different kind
travelling did

and I watched him
not sure what he had meant
but sure he had meant it
I think he meant travelling
replaced a different kind of pain
a pain of daily courtesy
a pain of unerring constancy
a pain of repeated devotion
the goddamned pain of love

and then he broke the silence
and said but yes
to answer your question
travelling was a bit of a pain
now that you ask

Visiting

On those visits to the very quiet
Houses, to the very tidy houses
Of carpet with no pile, Pan-O-Lux
Push sweepers standing ready, bookcases
Holding those well-bound issues of Guidepost,
Collected columns of Norman Vincent
Peale, scrapbooks of Little Nemo in
Wonderland, and underneath a handful
Of ancient games: Tiddly Winks with yellowed
Flaking instructions, a few metal Jacks,
The bounce gone from the ball, worn incomplete
Lincoln Logs smoothed from the many small hands
Of the many small years, an aged winking
Mr. Peanut of oiled hardwood, his
Hollowed limbs attached by sprung elastic,

I sat quietly immobile
paralyzed by sound
not listening to words
but to the comforting hum
of the cicada of kind inquiries
of health of friends and cousins
of deaths of old names
like Florence and Rhiney
and Esther and two Edwins
of old familial stories
recognized in my swoon
not from plot set-up punchline
but from the familiar singsong rhythm
the measured percussive
chuckles of ready anticipation
from the easy comfort of pauses
interludes that no one seemed to mind
the warm wash of hypnotic quiet
from the spaces between lives

Grandpa Sang From A Road Atlas

Grandpa sang from a road atlas
next to his easy chair
'Green Thing' Grandma called the chair
not so much out of fondness as spite
dragged it himself on to the back porch
no help none asked none needed
naught but the atlas he himself and Green Thing
and there he sat thumbing roads
Grandma refilling his big bowl of shell peanuts
out of the burlap bag from the feed store
during breaks from her great passion
Big Time Wrestling
Bobo Brazil versus The Sheik
No-Holds-Winner-Take-All-Death-Duel-Grudge-Match
sponsored by Pabst Blue Ribbon Beer

That Grandpa knew how to live
worked every sawmill on Pike's Peak
built houses and farmed dirt in Ohio
campaigned for Teddy in Ought-Four and beyond
intoning TR's name like 'Rose'
FDR's like 'Ruuuuse'"
drawn out and scrunched
as if he smelled something god awful
(never get him started on Harry Ass Truman)
knot on his forehead from flying cutoff
one leg longer than the other
three fingers missing from his working hand
through birth and accidents and life
bread balanced on the thumb and forefinger
wielded a hammer between the two
strong old lobster pinchers they were
thousands of nails that way
flicked matches and live cigar butts
into the trash can just to see her move fast
which she would not
not until the pitcher brimmed

even if the flames had burst
and licked the Stickley sideboard with white marble top
where her crystal bowl of Brach's
hard candies and equally hard caramels sat
complained of her jam pie
that's when the bottom crust's
jammed up agin the top crust
the only kind Grandma made and then burnt to boot
since from Pike's Peak to flat Ohio
she never really learned the egg timer
a long fall of pot roasts underdone
baked potatoes of mush
Sundays feared

but set aside saved and pressed
Edwardian engraved calling cards
delicate lace doilies
cardboard pages of gray unsmiling tintypes
had a son a bit too early on
the math just didn't work out right
and along the way among others a Half-Pint
and through the years debt dirt shoes or none
oranges for Christmas
bowled and bobbed haircuts every month no matter what
still to have an engraved card
white untattered pristine waiting
a bell a caller a civilized bow from the waist
ribbons hurriedly tied for a promenade
only a stroll Mother
out into a Saturday night
back soon
and then as lasting reward
Green Thing on the back porch
the roads strummed from memory
the years hummed just off tune

'62 Falcon

She didn't so much
stop at stop signs
as try to scare them
into early graves
and I being sole visitor
those summer weeks
and so honored
with the Seat of Death
spent those days splayed
on the unpadded dashboard
of Grandma's '62 Ford Falcon
braced with both hands
both feet
knees slightly bent
back arched
against the temerity of life

Late Summer, Ohio

Behind these end-season echoes
a wash of cicadas
applied with a stiff wide brush
their far-buzz a gesture
in slow easy arcs
repeated for the sake of technique
yes just to get it right
a chant-song
a death-rattle
the continuous chirp of forgiveness
cross the river on weathered planks
gapped as a shady old bridge
a soothe say the sayers
close the eyes only accept

The Children's Garden

Grief repeats like a radish. Or is it
Anticipatory? Before the fact?

As in this four by six. Glossy. Tattered.
There we all are, wide-eyed, on best behavior.
All lost souls. That was once the phrase.
In training. Though no one's a seer.

That one, there in the front row,
Hands in lap, trying to make
Himself small, trying on his lostness early.
It felt fine. Just fine.

And her, lingering there at the torn edge.
Unsure. A sad frown. Always that way,
If I remember. Gone by her own
Hand, I believe. A lost soul.

And the one in the middle, my best friend,
Looking surprised. Now, still
In prison. And for years to come, I've heard.
Unspeakable acts. I googled his mugshot.
No longer surprised. Resigned.

And what of the others? Blank pages
On to the end. Lost. Absence
Makes the heart heave harder.

Though if there's anyone, there's me.
There, in the back row. But here,
Now, preemptively found
Before I went missing. Now, held
In so many arms. Out of kindness, I suppose.
For my own good, likely as not.

Before I could go lost, a-wandering in woods,
Saved from wild feasting on peppered roots.

That Look

Here on this face I've either
seen before or not seen here
that particular lift of eyebrow
that bemused curl of lip
one pushing one tugging
recognized oh probably
since time since birth
oh definitely growing up with
living and dying with that arch
with that twist that said all you
needed to know of what she thought
of who were you kidding
of who did you think you were
oh come on now
it was enough and enough
was as good as a feast

Grain Elevators

From the fields then there was no vista
only rumored horizon
suspicious murmur of height
lives gridded in two dimensions
only the sun lucky to escape
and if faith failed and flat farmland swallowed
excreting a less than smaller version
if at some point in a pained existence
confirmation was necessitated
through youthful misdemeanor
you looked to the center of town
to those bastions over all staid acreage
lords of so many dusted rows beneath
towering keeps with monopolies on verticality
ramparts to be tested on off days off hours
off kilter from the fortunate sun
fathers' pickups shrinking below
both hands working heaven's rungs
rings of High Life hanging from belts
banging against youth-loins
giddy from the boldness of rascality
because if in your criminality you thought
there might be an actual elevator in this castle-keep
then you were sadly mistaken my friend

Small Town

The drawer hangs
right out the back
of the old wooden desk

right out the wall
out the side of the house
out into Main Street

the tight row of cancelled checks
the paid utility bills receipts
bank statements pipe cleaners

though there's nothing to see
for all to see
but look come see

(now is the time for the sighing)

Old Dog At The Red Apple Diner

I can't keep the names in the columns
who is the son who is the granddaughter
who is no relation
I treat them all as no relation
all friends all just friends

though I remember all the names at the Red Apple Diner
what shifts they work how tired they look
whether or not they worked last week
their own parents and grandparents
funny

oh I know it's funny
like the smear of sun I keep chasing around the house
first the sunroom then the study then the kitchen
a warm piece of light that keeps moving
like it's playing a joke on an old dog

Boy And A Button

He says to me I don't like things
where you just press a button
my friends have games and you
just press a button and that's it
there are board games even
where you just press a button
my dad says when he was a kid
you rolled dice and counted it out
counted money and pieces and read cards
now they make the games where
you just press a button my mom
even makes bread in a machine
and you just press a button
I'm not saying that's right
I'm not saying that's wrong
I just don't like it

and the whole time
he is winding thick
soiled string across his
two small hands a pirate
band-aid on each thumb
dirt under the nails
Cat's Cradle we used to call it
I watch the geometry
fine and beautiful
his little fingers weaving
exquisite patterns against
a bright blue sky no one
but him has ever noticed

Korea 1950-1953

I knew the veterans of that conflict
to be a bit lost
office managers and filling station owners
door-to-door salesmen and scoutmasters
brown shoes with drab green suits on Sunday
five o-clock shadow at eleven a.m.
tape on eyeglasses and missing gas caps
incomplete stacks of National Geographic
living rooms hung with the smell of bacon
cement blocks laying around to no good purpose
Blatz Beer and Tab Cola
the wait for checks to clear or rides to come
maybe a wife maybe not either way
owners of the ugliest dogs in America
dogs that would never come no matter
how loudly called
how insistently how pleadingly
they would just not come

Laurels Of Perseverance

These unfrayed shiny leaves
lose all weave and content
dropping singly by one and ones
scattering on all good winds
blowing free from anointed
heads touched heads crowned heads
well-scrubbed brows expecting
more than the simple long roads
the one right turn ahead
the other back left
on straight on straight
through dust and mournful heat
and beyond tedium as reward
the long slog into perpetuity
as we all fold into horizon

Screen Door

Your experience is in
no way my experience
so please just back away
from my screen door

yes I recognize your form
as loosely related to mine
but I ask again back away
from my screen door

your eyes shift your lips
move I should hear you
but only the howls of
the neighbor dog hold my ears

if I agree to feign interest
to nod apropos even to smile
will you then back away
from my screen door

here is my wallet here
is my breath my very soul
I will miss nothing only please
my screen door

Next

Assume too much, as usual, assume
You're in control, that those fabled better
Times lie ahead, that the bitter end is
Near, that the Reaper coming through the door
Is Grim. He's not. He's all cheap smirks and cracks,
An orange doughy face, the carny's patter.
Just don't stop scribbling whatever you do.
Motion him to the kitchen chair, the loose
Leg, the back that pops off, the cast iron
Stove with sharp corners directly behind.
Vague plans forms, high crimes certainly. Only
This: precious time will be gained to finish
This chapter, maybe start another one,
Before the next clown shows up, before all
Your best assumptions unravel again.

News Of The Day

My head grows smaller each day
fits easily into the palm
of my hand my fingers
wrap around meet under my chin
what does it hold
what can it anymore
short-sheeted stewings mistaken
for valid points of view
bitter loam piled thick on the tongue
a seethe of spit impossible to summon
admit nothing if pressed
everything if ignored

The Stars

So listen. Everyone's a pain in the ass.
The mother besieged by the son's troubles
Fondling a cross big enough to teeth on.
The widower wandering his yard in great
And devastating loss, the words to lay comfort
Hidden from all good neighbors.
The cancer patient tending her garden,
Large resonant woman in a muumuu
Sighing offkey to her adoring weeds.

Now lean in closer. For in much too short
A time we will no longer be able to see
The stars in the bright night above. Not for grit
Or grime or because of Edison
And his many patented tricks,
But because we will no longer think to look up,
No longer search the cornerless black,
No longer remember moments like now,
Sitting alone in observance, these
Little times stolen and rotating in pattern.

And just one thing more. The stars offer no pity
To us who fall so short. Still, we must try.
With nagging good cheer if possible.
With feeble whine if necessary.
With questions paid and silence returned.
All in the face of this cosmic *non grata*.
There is no other way.
And now is the time for the sighing.

Nap

Lay in opossum sleep
listen to the world outside
through open windows
try to fool yourself
that it's a different time
that the birds call from the future
that the winds whistle out of the past
that the sighs of the trees are meant
for a season other than this
try it   you can't do it

Dime Bottles And Cans

What will you do
To fill the hours without finish
When the audacious leisure takes hold?
The answer is there in your basket.

Keep peddling as you peddle now,
Down narrow gravel roads,
Along borders of a haunted country.
Keep stowing your little glories
With the dime bottles and cans:

The diving catch in leftfield at nine,
The girl who said yes at sixteen,
The planed door at forty-one
That fit after a long day's work,
But it fit, by Jesus,
Like a glove it fit.

Tractor Supply

"I believe I've traveled this road before . . ."
He let drop the steady quiet we had
Passed back and forth since starting out but then
Caught it with the same hand and brushed it off.
No harm done, none meant, and we continued
On again, our silence pouring from one
Side of the pickup to the other, gravel
Kicking the curves of the winding back roads.

So it continued to Tractor Supply,
The long judgments down lengths of lumber,
The standing-to at the ranks of nails,
The sliding of the tight silver coils
Into the bed of the pickup, only
The ringing of the register to scrape
Across our quiet task together, all
Without sign and all without subtitle.

Then back home along the same curving roads,
Passing that very same quiet we had
Always held so easily between us,
Until we turned up our own gravel drive
And stopped to look out at the field where
The fence would stand, the very same quiet
Leveling away into wind, until
He let go his grip again ". . . many times."

Patagonia

Scrambling to take the slack from her faults,
And I not arguing against graying
Sky and raking wind, she cursed insanely,
Stared wall-eyed, wailed high-pitched into the
Gales, *"Even Sisyphus . . . that anal
Retentive . . . hitched his shoulder differently . . .
On roll three-thousand two-hundred and ten . . ."*

On upward she climbed, not looking back,
While I, seeing the sun, fondled earth.
I paused as higher she rose, her last wisp
Indistinguishable from the spun
Cotton leavings in the sky,
*"Half the time . . . You try to convince yourself . . .
The other half . . . you just lie . . ."*

And what was resolved in this tautening,
This frenetic dash of self-improvement,
Everything left undone to cover
Or be covered for new season, new sun?

Sisyphus shifts weight more into his calves
With the pale hope that maybe this time
Before the stone stops, trembles, reverses,
Sisyphus double-timing just in front.

Wise Man

I know what it is to waste
to hurry past the single
cupped leaf filled with rainwater
to tip it carelessly on to sandy soil
nothing would have been sweeter
on my cracked lips
I know what it is
to throw away love
she would have done anything for me
she would have waited
to wait is Everything

he slapped thick varnish
for the bartender's attention
lifted his glass again
threw back his head

but this had been tried before

On The Trail

He lay in the woods for some time until
he couldn't tell how far they had come
or how long she had been gone
or how far up ahead she had walked
she never turned around
then as the sun rolled overhead
and he slept and he woke
slept and woke
he thought she came back to him
and stood over him
and was about to speak to him
but she turned and went on
wherever they had been walking in the first place
walking somewhere ever-where
he couldn't remember anymore
the trail so wide and soft
like their bed and the years mostly
then near dark he thought well
that's just fine fine fine
and he wasn't afraid or even cold
the things in the brush batted their eyes
as they watched over him
the crickets sang him to sleep then to wake
to sleep then to wake
the treetops parted and dark things drifted
this way and that
this way and that
down and turning until the wings of a crow
black and waxy
fluttered and fell over his eyes

Thanksgiving

Dear folks,
I thank you for your kind invite,
But I promise not to stay long.
It will be good to see your faces again,
Even get a good meal under my belt.
These years on the road have left me lean,
With less appetite than I once had.
I wonder if you'll even know me
From when we lost the place
And I went a little mad
And did not have the heart
To look for it again.
She never forgot it.
I know she would have enjoyed
Seeing your faces again, too,
Though that's past, the forgiving lost.
I guess the road has a way
Of changing us, when all is said
And spoken out to the end.
Myself, I find if I just wait a bit
The small things in the distance will
Get up beside me of their own pace.
I'm in no hurry anymore to run
And see what is over the next hill.
Sorry to say, that was her way in the end.
It only led to tears.
The road's long, after all.
Things will get here in time.
Like your kind invite.
I promise not to stay long.
Sincerely,

acknowledgments

*some poems have been previously published, in one form or another,
in the following publications:*

The Beatnik: Korea 1950-1953
Bird's Thumb: *And Yet; This Is What She Said She Saw*
Broad River Review: *Memory*
Connecticut Review: *Katterheinrich*
Crack the Spine: *Laurels of Perseverance; Tender Bits*
Euphony: *Tractor Supply*
Foliate Oak: *Screen Door; This Chill*
Inclement: *Hangers-On*
Indigo Rising: *February Loans*
Legendary: *Grandpa Sang From a Road Atlas; Patagonia: Visiting*
Margie: *Old Dog At the Red Apple Diner*
MockingHeart Review: *Something Like a River*
New Haven Review: *Business Trip*
New Plains Review: *Dime Bottles and Cans*
Penn Review: *Monster*
Plainsongs: *Nothingness*
Poet Lore: *Boy and a Button*
Poydras Review: *Leftover Sonnet*
Shot Glass Journal: *'62 Falcon*
Slice Magazine: *Song of the Horaltic*
Subliminal Interiors: *Judgment Day*
Third Wednesday: *Hollyhocks*
Tipton Poetry Journal: *In Which Mrs. Adams Observes and Passes Judgment
On the Cottonwood and the Goldfinch*
Twyckenham Notes: *O, Savagery; Panorama*

BD Feil is a writer who has lived around the Great Lakes all his life. Cleveland, Chicago, Michigan, now northwest Ohio. His stories and poems have been published in *Mississippi Review, Slice Magazine, Poet Lore, Craft Literary, Forge Literary, The Literateur, The Linnet's Wings, Mulberry Fork Review, New Haven Review, New Plains Review, Summerset Review,* and many other places. He writes deliberately, some might say slowly, yet steadily.